D1518592

TIMELINES OF
AMERICAN HISTORY™

A Timeline of the Life of George Washington

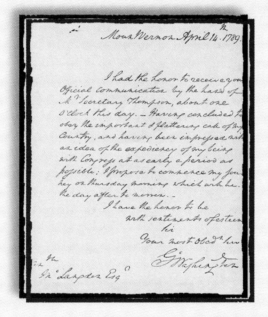

Vladimir Katz

The Rosen Publishing Group, Inc., New York

To my sister, OS-C, and the rest of my family, DVC, ALS, and MAS

Published in 2004 by The Rosen Publishing Group, Inc.
29 East 21st Street, New York, NY 10010

First Edition

Library of Congress Cataloging-in-Publication Data

Katz, Vladimir.
A timeline of the life of George Washington / Vladimir Katz.—1st ed.
    p. cm.—(Timelines of American history)
Summary: Provides a chronological look at the life and times of George Washington.
Includes bibliographical references and index.
ISBN 0-8239-4538-3 (lib. bdg.)
1. Washington, George, 1732–1799—Juvenile literature. 2. Washington, George,
1732–1799—Chronology—Juvenile literature. 3. Presidents—United States—Biography—
Juvenile literature. [1. Washington, George, 1732–1799. 2. Presidents. 3. United
States—History—Colonial period, 1600–1775. 4. United States—History—Revolution,
1775–1783.] I. Title. II. Series.
E312.66.K38 2004
973.4'1'092—dc22

        2003013936

Manufactured in the United States of America

On the cover: 1796 portrait of George Washington by Gilbert Stuart.
On the title page: Copy of a letter George Washington wrote to Congress accepting the presidency of the United States of America. Dated April 14, 1789, at Mount Vernon.

Contents

1
Early Life

Not much is known about George Washington's childhood. He had very little formal education. But he was good at math and at solving problems. George did not talk a lot, but he was a careful thinker. When he was young, the family moved around between his father's various farms in Virginia. George learned a lot about how to run a plantation. He also became skilled at trekking through the fields, rivers, and forests of the Virginia wilderness. George would always love nature and life on a farm.

This book's illustration shows young George Washington riding a horse. Also on the page but not shown are some lyrics to what became a popular patriotic song called "Yankee Doodle."

★ 1657

John Washington is the first Washington to come from England and settle in the colony of Virginia. The Washingtons become a respected family. They are involved in farming, buying and selling land, trading, and milling.

★ 1715

George's father, a successful farmer named Augustine Washington, marries Jane Butler, with whom he has four children.

★ 1731

Three years after the death of Jane Butler, Augustine Washington marries Mary Ball, George's mother.

★ 1732

George Washington is born on February 22, on

When George was a boy, he cut down his father's prized cherry tree. It became a famous story.

Wakefield Farm, in Virginia. He is the first of six children born to Mary and Augustine.

★ 1743

Augustine Washington dies. George is eleven years old. The farms owned by Augustine are left to George's mother and half brothers.

5

Coming of Age

During adolescence, George became a tall, strong, and athletic young man. As a teenager, George's role model was his older half brother Lawrence. Lawrence was a well-educated, sophisticated gentleman. When Augustine Washington died, Lawrence inherited Mount Vernon plantation. He began to build a magnificent mansion on the land. George's knowledge of the Virginia countryside and his many practical skills helped him get his first job.

George Washington loved Mount Vernon. It was very important to him. The land there totaled more than 8,000 acres and was divided into five farms. Washington designed the grounds to include wooded areas, meadows, walkways, and an herb garden.

★ 1748

At age fifteen, George Washington gets his first job. He is hired as an assistant to a group of field surveyors who work for Lord Fairfax. Fairfax, a wealthy neighbor of Lawrence Washington's, owns a great deal of land in northern Virginia.

★ 1749

Washington becomes a surveyor of Culpepper County, in Virginia. He explores, measures, and writes accounts of parts of the wilderness. These accounts contain important information about the land, which helps it be bought, sold, and settled by farmers.

This image shows Washington working as a land surveyor.

★ 1751

Washington travels to the Caribbean island of Barbados with Lawrence. He catches smallpox, a disease that leaves permanent marks—pocks—on his face.

★ 1752

Lawrence Washington dies.

2

A Soldier and a Planter

After surveying for a few years, George Washington began a military career. Because he knew the Virginia wilderness well, he joined British forces when Britain went to war against the French and their Indian allies. At the time, Britain ruled the American colonies. In the early 1750s, the British and French were fighting for land in the Ohio Valley. During the French and Indian War, Washington earned an excellent reputation. Because of this, he was made commander of all Virginia troops.

George Washington at age twenty-five

1752
Washington inherits Mount Vernon's 2,000 acres from his half brother Lawrence.

1754
As a lieutenant colonel, Washington fights the first battles of the French and Indian War. Washington is a very good soldier. He is so brave, daring, and resourceful that he earns a reputation all over the colonies and even in Europe.

This battle scene from 1854 shows George Washington during the French and Indian War. Washington is commanding from his horse while his soldiers fight during the Battle of the Monongahela. In the two-hour battle, during which sixty-three men died, Washington was the only one of the eighty-six British and American officers who was not shot down.

1755 ★

Washington becomes an aide (assistant) to British general Edward Braddock. During battle, he narrowly escapes death.

1758 ★

Washington is promoted to a general and plays an important role in helping British troops defeat the French. His troops admire and respect him because he always looks out for his soldiers. Later in the year, he happily returns to Mount Vernon.

Martha Washington

George Washington met and fell in love with a woman named Martha Dandridge Custis. They lived at Mount Vernon. Plantation

Martha Washington

life was difficult because the British king forced American planters to follow many unfair rules. Americans became angry by what they viewed as unreasonable practices. For instance, Washington could not sell his own tobacco. He had to ship it to England, where merchants sold it for him. After charging whatever price they wanted, the merchants kept part of the profits. As a result, although he worked hard, Washington had a difficult time making a living.

George Washington

★ July 26, 1757

When she is twenty-six, Martha Dandridge Custis's first husband, a wealthy planter named Daniel Park Custis, suddenly dies.

★ 1758

Washington meets the recently widowed Martha. She has two children from her first marriage: John, known as Jacky, and Martha, who is called Patsy. Two other children, Daniel and Frances, died as infants.

Washington becomes a member of the Virginia House of Burgesses, a democratically elected group of landowners that governs the colony of Virginia.

★ January 6, 1759

George Washington marries Martha Dandridge Custis. With her children, Martha moves to Mount Vernon. Washington adopts Jacky and Patsy.

The wedding of George Washington and Martha Dandridge Custis took place on January 6, 1759. In April of the same year, George, Martha, and her two children from her first marriage moved into Mount Vernon.

3

The American Revolution

Throughout the 1750s, American colonists became more and more angry with the new laws the British government kept creating. The colonists thought these laws—called acts—were unfair. First England insisted that Americans could buy only English products. Then England put very high taxes on these products. George Washington and other colonists became more and more rebellious. They protested many of these laws, including the Sugar Act, the Stamp Act, the Townshend Acts, and the Tea Act.

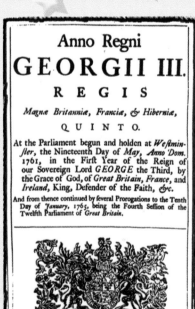

Anno Regni
GEORGII III.
REGIS
Magnæ Britanniæ, Franciæ, & Hiberniæ,
QUINTO.

At the Parliament begun and holden at *Westminster*, the Nineteenth Day of *May*, *Anno Dom.* 1761, in the First Year of the Reign of our Sovereign Lord *GEORGE* the Third, by the Grace of God, of *Great Britain, France*, and *Ireland*, King, Defender of the Faith, *&c.*

And from thence continued by several Prorogations to the Tenth Day of *January*, 1765, being the Fourth Session of the Twelfth Parliament of *Great Britain*.

LONDON:
Printed by *Mark Baskett*, Printer to the King's most Excellent Majesty; and by the Assigns of *Robert Baskett*. 1765.

This is the title page of the first edition of the Stamp Act, which was created by the English government in January 1765. The entire document was twenty-five pages long—in small print. This was the very first direct tax that Britain imposed of its colonies in America. Britain's hope was that such a tax would help the government make back some of the money it had spent on troops in the colonies. Even newspapers were taxed!

★ 1764

England passes the Sugar Act, which places taxes on items such as sugar, coffee, and fabric.

★ 1765

England passes the Stamp Act, which taxes anything printed on paper. Washington and Virginia's government protest this tax.

★ 1767

England passes the Townshend Acts, which add taxes to items such as tea, paper, and glass.

★ 1770

The Boston Massacre occurs when British soldiers shoot at a crowd of protesting colonists. Five people are killed.

Boston Tea Party

★ 1773

England passes the Tea Act, which places high taxes on tea. Angry colonists protest by dumping tea into Boston Harbor. This event is known as the Boston Tea Party.

★ 1774

The British close Boston Harbor until colonists pay for the ruined tea.

A New Government

George Washington believed that many of these new British laws and acts were part of England's plan to take away the colonies' independent governments. With other Virginia burgesses, or state government representatives, Washington organized the Continental Congress. Representatives from all thirteen American colonies met in

This image shows General George Washington standing up in the Assembly Room of the State House (now called Independence Hall) in Philadelphia, Pennsylvania. Here, on June 15, 1775, Washington was appointed as commander in chief of the Continental army of the colonies.

Philadelphia. They decided that they would no longer buy British goods and no longer pay taxes.

The Continental Congress became a new government. Its members were prepared to resist British rule. With all his military experience, Washington was chosen to organize independent military groups that could fight against British troops in case there was a war.

★ **1774**
Britain outlaws the members of Virginia's House of Burgesses from holding public meetings.

Washington is chosen as one of Virginia's representatives at the First Continental Congress that meets in Philadelphia in September.

★ **May 10, 1775**
The Second Continental Congress meets in Philadelphia. Washington is one of the representatives from Virginia.

★ **June 1775**
Washington is elected commander in chief of the newly created Continental army. On July 3, he takes charge of the first American army. They have not had good training, and they are poorly equipped.

15

War of Independence

In 1776, Washington joined members of the Continental Congress in Philadelphia to sign the Declaration of Independence. The document declared that the thirteen colonies would now be an independent American nation. However, true freedom would come only when the American colonists had won it from the British. After six long and difficult years of war, Washington led his troops to victory. This was quite amazing since the British had more men and were better armed.

★ **1776**
Shortly after the Declaration of Independence is adopted on July 4, the British attack the colonists. The war for independence is on. The Declaration is signed on August 2.

★ **1777**
During a freezing winter, Washington's army stays at Valley Forge. Many die from hunger, cold, and illness.

★ **1778**
France sends money and troops to help Washington's army.

Glossary

allies (A-lyz) Countries that support or help one another.

Articles of Confederation (AR-tih-kulz UV kun-feh-deh-RAY-shun) First set of guidelines written for the United States government.

burgesses (BUR-jis-is) White landowners who were elected as representatives to Virginia's colonial government.

constitution (kon-stih-TOO-shun) A country's written system of rules that outlines the powers and duties of the government and protects citizens' rights.

Continental Congress (kon-tin-EN-tul KON-gres) America's first government made up of elected representatives from each of the thirteen colonies.

Declaration of Independence (deh-kluh-RAY-shun UV in-duh-PEN-dints) Document in which the thirteen colonies declare independence from Britain and describe their desires for a new American nation.

estate (is-TAYT) A piece of property or land with a large house on it.

executive (ek-ZEH-kyuh-tiv) Dealing with the running of a country and the putting into practice of a country's laws. The executive branch of the U.S. government is the president.

A Timeline of the Life of George Washington

Founding Fathers (FOWN-ding FA-therz) Group of famous
Americans who together created an independent, democratic
American government.

judicial (joo-DIH-shul) Dealing with justice and the fairness of laws.
The judicial branch of the U.S. government is the Supreme Court.

legislative (LEH-jis-lay-tiv) Dealing with the making of laws. The
legislative branch of the U.S. government is Congress.

milling (MIH-ling) The process of grinding grain into flour or meal.

neutral (NOO-trul) To take no sides (in a conflict).

oath (OHTH) A serious promise.

rebellion (ruh-BEL-yun) An angry rising up against authority or power.

rebellious (ruh-BEL-yus) To resist authority.

resourceful (rih-SORS-ful) Good at thinking of ways to do things.

surrender (suh-REN-der) To give up.

surveyor (ser-VAY-er) Someone whose job is to take measurements
of a piece of land and map the land on paper.

trekking (TREH-king) Walking over difficult ground.

Virginia House of Burgesses (ver-JIN-ya HOWS UV BUR-jis-is)
America's first government made up of elected representatives
(burgesses) of the colony of Virginia.

widow (WIH-doh) A woman whose husband has died.

At the Constitutional Convention, which began on May 25 and ended on September 17, 1787, the American Constitution was written. The Constitution created a strong federal government made up of three equally important branches: executive (the president), legislative (Congress), and judicial (the Supreme Court).

1787 ★

With Washington as leader of the Constitutional Convention, the Founding Fathers write the United States Constitution in Philadelphia, Pennsylvania.

1788 ★

Nine out of thirteen American states approve the Constitution, making it the supreme law of the land.

The New President

After the War of Independence, George Washington wanted to return to his family and his farm at Mount Vernon. Instead, in 1789, he was elected the first president of the United States. During the Revolution years, Washington had basically been the leader of the independent nation. He knew much about its land and people and supported democratic ideas. Because of his

Washington was inaugurated as president in Old City Hall (later called Federal Hall) in New York City on April 30, 1789. On April 14, 1789, he was at Mount Vernon when Charles Thompson, the secretary of the Continental Congress, arrived with a letter saying that Washington had been elected president.

views, talents, and popularity, many thought he would be a perfect president.

The members of Washington's first cabinet included two other important Founding Fathers: Thomas Jefferson and Alexander Hamilton.

★ **1789**

George Washington is elected the first president of the United States of America. He is sworn in on April 30, in the nation's first capital, New York City. Crowds cheer as he takes the presidential oath on the balcony of Old City Hall. Washington appoints Thomas Jefferson and Alexander Hamilton to his cabinet.

★ **1790**

The nation's capital moves to Philadelphia, where it stays for ten years.

★ **1791**

The Bill of Rights is added to the Constitution. Its amendments list the basic rights of all American citizens. Washington chooses the swamplands around the Potomac River as the site of a new capital. In his honor, it is named Washington, D.C.

The Bill of Rights

21

Nation Building

As the United States's first leaders, Washington and his government had to build a country from scratch. They set to work creating many of the American systems and institutions that still exist today. They developed the nation's justice system and the Supreme Court as well as tax, banking, financial, and postal systems. Washington's government concentrated on opening up the West. By the end of 1795, the United States had extended its territories to the Mississippi River.

1789
The Judiciary Act creates the nation's justice system. The Tariff Act and the Tonnage Act are the first laws of a new tax system. The government operates with the tax money paid by citizens.

1790
The nation's highest court of justice, the Supreme Court, hears its first case.

1791
The Bank Act outlines a national banking system.

1792
Washington is reelected as president. The federal post office and the New York Stock Exchange are created. The Coinage Act allows the federal government to produce coins.

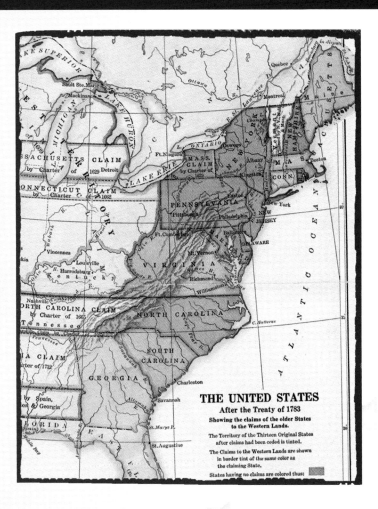

This map shows what land was part of the United States of America after the treaty of 1783.

THE UNITED STATES
After the Treaty of 1783
Showing the claims of the older States
to the Western Lands.
The Territory of the Thirteen Original States
after claims had been ceded is tinted.
The Claims to the Western Lands are shown
in border tint of the same color as
the claiming State.
States having no claims are colored thus:

⭐ 1793

War breaks out between England and France. Since Washington is for peace and against war, the United States remains neutral.

⭐ 1795

An agreement with Spain gives the United States the right to sail boats along the Mississippi River.

23

Final Years

Washington did not want to be elected for a third term as president. His decision became a tradition in American politics. With the exception of Franklin Delano Roosevelt, no president has served more than two terms (eight years). This two-term maximum became law as the Twenty-second Amendment to the Constitution. Having retired, Washington returned to Mount Vernon. Three years later, he died on his farm.

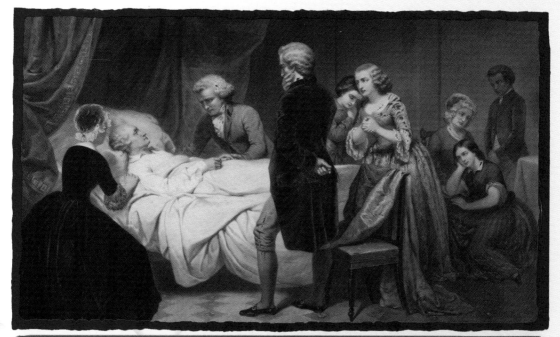

This lithograph shows the deathbed of George Washington. On December 13, 1799, Washington was in a sleet storm and he caught a cold. The next morning, the doctor was sent for. Washington's last words later that evening were, "I am dying, sir—but am not afraid to die."

1795

Washington poses for the portrait that is now on the $1 bill.

1796

Tired of politics and the conflicts between two new parties that would later become the Republicans and the Democrats, Washington gives his farewell speech. He returns to Mount Vernon.

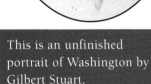

This is an unfinished portrait of Washington by Gilbert Stuart.

1799

While working on his plantation, Washington comes down with a severe cold. He dies on December 14 of a throat infection. For months, the nation mourns its first president, one of the most important figures in American and world history.

George Washington played major roles in three of the most important events in U.S. history: the War of Independence, the writing of the Constitution, and the building of a new democratic nation dedicated to the rights of all men.

Mount Vernon

When he retired from being president, George Washington was glad to return to his life as a tobacco farmer at Mount Vernon. As he once said, "No estate in America is more pleasantly situated than [Mount Vernon]." He also admitted that he would "rather be at home at Mount Vernon with a friend or two" than be in Washington, D.C., or in a meeting with all the kings and presidents of Europe.

During the past twenty-five years, the Mount Vernon Ladies' Association has been hard at work restoring Washington's famous home. The estate is open to visitors every day.

Martha Washington also much preferred the simpler life of Mount Vernon to the formal life she had led as America's first first lady.

1799
By the time of his death, Washington has expanded Mount Vernon to five working farms, a main mansion built of pine, and a series of gardens and walkways.

1802
Martha dies on May 22 from a severe fever. She is buried next to her husband at Mount Vernon.

1858
George Washington's great-grandnephew, John A. Washington III, can no longer afford to keep Mount Vernon running. The house and surrounding land are sold to the Mount Vernon Ladies' Association. Today, it is the most visited historic home in the United States after the White House.

Visitors are standing outside the brick tomb of George and Martha Washington at Mount Vernon.

27

Using Timelines to Show Relationships

Timelines can be very helpful for people studying history. They provide an outline of important events organized according to the years in which they happened. Events are ordered from the earliest to the most recent. In one look, you can easily see what happened and when. You can also discover how one event led to another over a long period of time. Timelines give you basic facts and dates that serve as useful guides when you need to research individual subjects in more depth.

Web Sites

Due to the changing nature of Internet links, the Rosen Publishing Group, Inc., has developed an online list of Web sites related to the subject of this book. This site is updated regularly. Please use this link to access the list.

http://www.rosenlinks.com/tah/gwas

Index

A Timeline of the Life of George Washington

Credits

About the Author: Vladimir Katz lives in Astoria, New York.

Photo credits: cover © Museum of the City of New York/Corbis; p. 1 © Library of Congress; pp. 4, 5, 7, 8, 12 © 2003 Picture History LLC; p. 6 © Joseph Martin/ Album/Yale University, New Haven/Art Archive; pp. 9, 11, 24, 25 © Library of Congress Prints and Photographs Division; pp. 10 (left and right), 14, 17, 19, 23 © Hulton Archive/Getty Images; p. 13 © Corbis; p. 20 © Bettmann/Corbis; p. 21 © General Records of the United States Government; Record Group 11; National Archives; p. 26 © James P. Blair/Corbis; p. 27 © Wolfgang Kaehler/Corbis.

Designer: Geri Fletcher; Editor: Annie Sommers